FIRST GOSPEL SINGER

I0800671

IRA SANKEY
FIRST GOSPEL SINGER

BY BETTY STEELE EVERETT

CHRISTIAN • LITERATURE • CRUSADE
Fort Washington, Pennsylvania 19034

CHRISTIAN LITERATURE CRUSADE
U.S.A.
P.O. Box 1449, Fort Washington, PA 19034

with publishing programs also in:
GREAT BRITAIN
51 The Dean, Alresford, Hants., SO24 9BJ

AUSTRALIA
P.O. Box 419M, Manunda, QLD 4879

NEW ZEALAND
10 MacArthur Street, Feilding

ISBN 0-87508-471-0

Copyright © 1999
Betty Steele Everett

Photographs used with permission from:

The Lawrence County Historical Society,
408 N. Jefferson St. P.O. Box 1745
New Castle, PA. 16103
&
The Billy Graham Center Museum,
Wheaton College, Wheaton, IL 60187

Text set in Gilde
Titles set in Oxford

Cover design by Skip Mable Studio

This printing 1999

ALL RIGHTS RESERVED

Printed in the United States of America

Contents

Illustrations

Chapter

1

Growing Up in Pennsylvania

"IT'S A BOY!" Although David and Mary Sankey were proud of their new son, whom they named Ira David, no one else in the little western Pennsylvania town of Edinburg saw anything unusual or particularly promising in him. He was just a new baby boy in town.

It was August 23, 1840. Martin Van Buren was President, but running against him now was William Henry Harrison. Harrison was reminding everyone of how he had put down an Indian uprising twenty-nine years earlier at Tippecanoe, Indiana, his slogan being "Tippecanoe and Tyler, too." Tyler was running with him for Vice-President.

The Sankey family, of Scotch-Irish background, was a good one for a baby to be born into. David

Sankey was a state legislator, and his family could afford many of the luxuries of the day. The family was also staunch Methodist and was musically gifted.

Ira would follow their example and one day become the most outstanding evangelistic singer in America.

Almost from birth, Ira heard his mother singing. As he got older he joined the family around the log fire during the winter months to sing away the long dark evenings. They sang all the hymns they had learned at church; it was the only music they knew.

Although Ira never had any formal musical training, he quickly learned to read music and to play both the piano and organ.

It was the music and singing at church that made Ira eager to go each week—not the long, and sometimes dull, sermons. He also went to Sunday school in an old schoolhouse, but he did not become a Christian until he was 16 years old.

That year he went to revival meetings held at King's Chapel Methodist Church, about three miles from his home, and there he gave his life to Christ.

The next year another big change took place in the Sankeys' lives.

"I've been offered the position of president of the Bank of New Castle," Ira's father said. "It means we'll have to move there, but it will be worth it. And it is only five miles away."

New Castle, north and slightly west of Pittsburgh, was bigger than Edinburg and more "modern." The new bank president and his family would be important, respected citizens.

Once in New Castle, Ira began high school and also joined the Methodist Episcopal church. His strong voice and musical talent were quickly noticed, and he was appointed church choir director.

After he graduated from high school, Ira did the expected thing—he went to work as a clerk in his father's bank.

Now he began to get more involved in the church. He served as Sunday school superintendent, taught a Sunday school class, and continued to direct the choir.

Soon he began studying the Bible so he could teach a large class of men and women once a week in the "way of holiness." It gave him a firm basis in the Scriptures, which would come to good use in the future. He was 20 years old.

Ira was a good-looking young man, with black hair and eyes that turned women's heads. He was always neatly dressed and had an easygoing way about him that made him popular with everyone he met.

Most things about the choir and its music pleased Ira—except for the fact that no musical instruments were allowed in the church to accompany the choir. Instruments, other than the human voice, were thought to be "worldly" and "wicked."

"It's all right to twang a tuning fork on the back of a hymnbook," Ira was told, "but anything else is a sin! It should be just voice, pure and simple, praising the Lord!"

Although Ira decided to work to change things, it was several years before he convinced a majority of the church members that using a small organ to help the choir singers was not a sin, but would actually improve their praise to God. He finally won.

When the organ was set up, it was quickly agreed that Ira should be the first one to play it at a service.

"Some people have threatened to walk out if you play an instrument," he was warned, but Ira had no intention of stopping now.

As he played, Sankey kept an eye on the congregation. Sure enough, one or two members did get up and stalk out in protest, but most stayed to hear the choir sing for the first time with organ accompaniment.

With the organ now firmly installed in the church service, Ira began to make more use of his voice, singing wherever and whenever he had the opportunity. He sang both locally and in other cities and states. It was good experience for his future, although at this point he knew only that he enjoyed singing for the Lord and that people enjoyed listening to him.

Ira's father, noticing how often Ira was away, singing at conventions and religious meetings, told Mary, "I'm afraid that boy will never amount to anything! All he does is run around the country with a hymnbook under his arm!"

Mary replied sharply, "I'd rather see him with a hymnbook under his arm than with a whiskey bottle in his pocket."

In 1861 the growing tension between the northern and southern states erupted into war, despite everything some people had done to try to prevent it. Compromises and even the Mason-Dixon Line had not kept war from finally coming.

"Fort Sumter's been taken," Ira told his parents. "President Lincoln's called for Army volunteers, and I'm going to enlist. I'll be part of Company B of the 22nd Regiment of the Pennsylvania volunteers."

Joining the army must have seemed more like going to a family reunion to Ira. The lieutenant and first sergeant were members of the larger Sankey family, and well known to the singer. Ira himself was a sergeant, and his brother Richard was a corporal.

Ira and his company were sent to Maryland, where they camped along the Gunpowder River.

In camp, Ira turned to what he loved to do best: sing and lead others in singing. Sitting around the campfires in the evening, someone would say, "Start a song, Sankey," and in his rich baritone, Ira would begin.

The men, hungry for something to do, homesick already for what they'd left behind and unsure of their future, joined in. They loved Ira and his music, and he was popular because of it.

Although Maryland stayed in the Union, it still had a southern "flavor" and outlook. Many of the people resented the Union soldiers, but it didn't take long for the people near the camp to hear about the singing of "The Boys in Blue." They began to invite Ira and the soldiers who sang with him into their homes.

Ira chose songs everyone knew, and his piano playing and the men's singing helped to make both the local people and the soldiers feel better about each other. It was easier to become friends when they sang together, even though they didn't agree on politics.

Company B did not see any action while Ira was with them, and when his enlistment time was up, he went back to New Castle to pick up his old life and routine.

Although Ira had been in the army only the three months for which he had enlisted, President Lincoln had made David Sankey the Internal Revenue collector in New Castle while Ira was gone. Now the veteran became his father's helper. He also went back to directing the church choir and singing at conventions and other gatherings.

While Ira liked and was friendly with all the members of the choir, one young woman took his eye in a special way.

"I'm going to ask Miss Fanny Edwards to marry me," Ira decided.

Fanny was a good choice. Her father was a state senator, and the family was highly respected throughout the state.

Fanny accepted Ira's proposal, and the wedding was on September 9, 1863. Now Ira began the life of a small-town American husband, content to live a quiet, moderate life, working at a safe, comfortable, and well-paying job. Mr. and Mrs. Ira David Sankey seemed set for life in New Castle, Pennsylvania.

As time went on, as part of his community and Christian interests, Ira helped to organize a YMCA in the city. His popularity helped him get elected secretary, first, and then president.

It was this YMCA position that would be instrumental in changing Ira's small-town life into one that would make his name—and music—known among Christians around the world.

Courtesy LCHS

King's Chapel Church (Methodist) was founded in 1803. This building, the third on this location, was built in 1856 and it was here that Ira Sankey, at age 16, professed his Christian faith. This church has been replaced by a new structure at a nearby location.

Chapter

2

A Meeting with D.L. Moody . . . and Destiny

AS THE HEAD of the New Castle YMCA, a position Sankey had held almost since he helped start the chapter, he was a delegate to the National Convention in 1870. The convention was scheduled for Indianapolis, Indiana, and Ira was excited about the possibility of going.

"Dwight L. Moody is to be there, too," he told Fanny, "and I've heard and read so much about him that I want to meet him. He's a dynamic evangelist."

Stories of Moody and his methods of evangelism in Chicago's inner city were well known. He had begun the North Market Sunday School with the "hoodlums" from the streets, and now it had grown to be one of the largest in the city.

President Lincoln had shown his admiration for Moody's work by visiting the school on his way to Washington to start his first term as president.

Some of Moody's ways seemed radical to the minds of the more staid and formal ministers in the city. He had bought a pony that he led around the North Side of Chicago. A pony in the city was bound to attract attention, especially for the children Moody wanted to reach for Christ. Often the pony would be almost covered with children, while others ran alongside, hoping for a turn to ride. With each step, Moody was leading them to his mission school.

While Sankey had heard much about Moody, he did not know that the evangelist had heard of him, too, and was looking for a song leader for his services.

During the first days of the convention the two did not meet. Moody was there with the Chicago delegation, Sankey with the New Castle men, and the groups had been assigned to sit in different parts of the hall.

Then, on Saturday afternoon, it was announced that Moody would lead a 6 a.m. Sunday morning prayer meeting at the Baptist Church. Sankey thought it might be his last chance to meet the evangelist.

The next morning Sankey got to the meeting late, and had to sit near the door in the back. A few minutes later a man leaned over to whisper, "Mr. Sankey, the singing here has been abominable. I wish you would start up something when that man stops praying, if he ever does."

When "that man" gave the final "Amen," Sankey began singing "There Is a Fountain Filled with Blood." Eagerly, the congregation joined in, and the song boomed out over the crowd. After the meeting, the man who had asked Sankey to sing introduced him to Moody.

Moody was a short, well-built man. His large head, short neck, and rounded but wide shoulders would have looked at home on an NFL lineman. His dark hair came over his forehead, and his eyes were big and expressive. He had a well-kept beard and a laugh that made everyone who heard it want to laugh, too.

Sankey was also a big man, but actually he and Moody looked nothing alike. Sankey was more handsome than the evangelist and was always impeccably dressed. Moody tended to be more on the rugged side and not always so neatly dressed.

Moody grasped Sankey's hand, and later Ira would say the evangelist looked into his eyes as though looking into his soul.

"Where are you from?" Moody demanded in his usual take-charge style.

"New Castle, Pennsylvania."

"Are you married?" Moody went on.

Sankey nodded. "With two boys."

"What is your business?"

"I'm a government official with the Internal Revenue Service in New Castle."

"Well, you'll have to give it up!" Moody announced.

"Give up my job? What for?"

Sankey did not explain that there would be a pension for him later when he was old enough to retire, and his job was a secure one that he wouldn't be fired from. Both he and the position were respected around the whole area. He was quite satisfied with his life, his work, his family, and New Castle.

"To come to Chicago and help me in my work!" Moody told him.

"I can't do that!" Sankey protested. "I can't just up and move to Chicago!"

"You have to! I've been looking for you for the past eight years!"

Moody was tone deaf, a monotone singer who could hardly hit a right note, although he had learned to cover it in his services. But he had long realized the effect a good song leader had on an audience. He wanted a "co-worker in song."

Sankey hesitated. The thought of working with Moody was exciting, but he was sure he could not leave his job and move to Chicago. Right now he just wanted Moody to let up on him.

"I'll pray about it," he promised.

"Good! Let's pray right now!" Moody led the way to a private area, and Sankey followed—more out of politeness than anything else.

While Sankey was impressed with Moody's prayer, he still did not feel he wanted to move to Chicago.

The next day Sankey got a card from Moody, asking him to meet him that evening at 6 o'clock on a certain street corner for an open-air meeting.

Sankey scribbled "I'll be there," and handed the card back to the messenger.

With a few friends, Sankey went to the address Moody had given him. The evangelist was already there. Without greeting Sankey, Moody went into a store on the corner, and in a minute came back with a big box.

"We'll use this." Moody rolled the box to the side of the street, then stood up on it and turned to Sankey. "Sing 'Am I a Soldier of the Cross?'"

Sankey did as ordered. It was the end of a long working day in the mills in the neighborhood, and the men were on their way home, swinging their lunch pails. It didn't take more than a couple of hymns before a large crowd had gathered around the box, eager for the excitement of something different after their dull, tiring day.

The talk Moody gave impressed Sankey. The crowd stood still, almost hypnotized by the fiery words that poured out of Moody's mouth. Some men wiped tears from their eyes as they listened.

After he had spoken to the men for about twenty minutes, Moody closed with a short prayer.

"I'm holding another meeting right away at the Opera House," Moody told the crowd. "You're all invited to come along to it with me."

At Moody's signal, Sankey began to sing "Shall We Gather at the River?" The men, eager to hear more, fell into line and marched down the street behind the two leaders.

At the Opera House, Moody made sure all the men with him had found seats on the first floor before he got up on the platform to speak.

Moody preached until the YMCA delegates began to come in for the evening session of the convention. With a prayer, Moody ended the service, telling the men to go home now and get something to eat.

"It's time for the brethren of the convention to talk over the question 'How to Reach the Masses,'" Moody ended with a smile.

While the offer to come to work with Moody was exciting and a tribute to his singing and leadership ability, Sankey was still not sure the Lord was calling him to give up his comfortable lifestyle and his work with the church and its choir, and move his family to Chicago. He went home without promising anything.

Fanny, too, was not convinced when Ira explained the offer to her. "It's too much to ask," she said, shaking her head.

Neither Ira nor Fanny appreciated Moody's keeping at them. For the next six months the evangelist kept urging Sankey to join him. Finally Ira gave in and agreed to spend just one week with Moody in Chicago.

Sankey took the train to Chicago, arriving in the Windy City just about dawn. He grabbed a quick breakfast, then headed for Moody's home on the North Side.

"Come in," Moody invited, and led the way to the organ. Although the family was gathered for morning prayers, Moody did not introduce any of them. Instead, he told Sankey, "Sit down at the organ and lead the singing for our family devotions."

Sankey may have been surprised, but he did as he was told. Only after the devotions did Moody introduce his family, including his wife, Emma, who had married Moody when she was just 19.

"I have a busy day planned for us," Moody told Sankey. "First, I am going to visit a lot of sick people and I want you to come with me and sing for them."

In the first home they visited the mother was ill. Moody told her he would read from the Bible to her, but first Mr. Sankey was going to sing. The hymn Sankey chose was a popular one of that time, "Scatter Seeds of Kindness."

Strangely, this first hymn Sankey sang while actually working with Moody was also the last one he sang when the two held their last public meeting twenty-eight years later in Brooklyn. Of course, neither man had any idea of this at the time.

The rest of that week Sankey helped Moody in meetings in the Illinois Street Church that Moody had begun, at noon prayer meetings in the business section of the city, and at some evangelistic meetings in various churches. The week ended with a big meeting in Farwell Hall, the YMCA building in downtown Chicago.

During that last meeting, as the congregation sang the opening hymn, Moody whispered to Sankey, "I am going to speak on 'The Prodigal Son.' I want you to sing one of the songs you sang in Indianapolis, 'Come Home, O Prodigal Child.'"

Sankey shook his head. "I can't. There's no organ to accompany myself on." Sankey was used to accompanying himself on a small organ called a harmonium.

Moody pointed to a big organ at the back of the platform that had cost $3,000, a huge sum in those days. "Isn't that big enough for you?"

Sankey saw immediately that while the organ was big, it was really too big and too far away. If he played it while he sang, he would have his back to the audience, making it hard to be effective. He also doubted if the regular organist could accompany him the way he wanted.

"Give him a book and tell him how you want him to play it," Moody said.

Sankey did, and Moody gave his sermon. At the end, he turned to Sankey, telling the congregation, "Now Mr. Sankey will sing a solo for us. Let it be perfectly still while he sings."

Sankey got up, turning to signal the organist that he was ready, but there was no one at the organ. The organist, following his usual habit, had slipped out for a smoke while Moody preached and was not back yet!

It took only a few seconds for Sankey to see what he had to do. He stepped to the front of the platform and began to sing with no accompaniment. Moody was delighted!

The next morning Moody took Sankey to the train for his trip home to New Castle.

"You see, I was right!" the evangelist said enthusiastically. "Your singing has been very helpful to all the meetings, and I am sure you should give up your business and come to Chicago at once!"

At home, Sankey was again torn about what the Lord wanted him to do. He had enjoyed the week he had spent working with Moody, but he also knew if he and his family moved to Chicago it would mean going on faith. And, he told himself, he was already serving the Lord with his music and in his church.

Sankey decided to talk to his pastor. He was secretly hoping he would be told not to leave New Castle, but instead his pastor urged him to go.

Other friends whom he asked for advice all told him it was his duty to go to Chicago, and finally Sankey had to surrender.

His resignation was accepted by the Secretary of the Treasury. His job was given, on Sankey's recommendation, to a soldier who had escaped from a Confederate prison during the war.

Moody and Sankey were now a team.

Courtesy LCHS

Bird's eye view of New Castle, 1871

Courtesy LCHS

East Washington Street 1907, looking west from near East Street, Note the utility poles supporting dozens of wires.

Chapter

3

Burned Out in Chicago

SANKEY BEGAN his work with Moody in Chicago in early 1871. He was a less aggressive person than Moody and was content to let the evangelist dominate the partnership in many ways.

Yet both men had an ability to get along with people, and they were in agreement on keeping both the talks and the singing "simple." Also, they were both dedicated to using their individual talents to win people to Christ. All this let them blend into a good working relationship.

Moody's family was already living on the north side of the city, but Sankey was alone, not wanting to move Fanny and the children to Chicago until he was sure of what would come from working with Moody.

The two men spent their days singing and praying with the sick, singing and talking (Moody never liked to think he "preached") at the daily noon prayer meetings and other services, including Sunday evening ones in Farwell Hall.

Everything went smoothly for them until the evening service on October 8, 1871.

The weather had been blistering hot, and air conditioning was unheard of, so church and meeting attendance had been down for some time.

In September, to try to get people back, Moody had decided to preach on Bible characters.

The idea worked, and on this night the biggest crowd ever was in the Hall. "What shall I do with Jesus?" was Moody's subject: the fifth in a series of six he had planned on the life of Jesus.

As usual at the end of his talk, Moody asked Sankey to sing. By the time Ira got to the third verse of "Today the Savior Calls," his voice was drowned out by the wailing of fire sirens, and the noise of the horse-drawn engines rushing by the building. Bells began to toll, as well.

"That's the great City Bell," Sankey realized as he heard the distinctive deep tones of the bell in the old courthouse steeple. "That means a general alarm!" Now everyone knew something serious was wrong in the city.

It was actually the start of the historic Chicago fire that would burn from that night until the 11th of the month, destroying one-third of the city—17,000 buildings—and doing $197 million in damage.

Quickly Moody closed the meeting, and the people rushed to join the confusion already in the streets.

"Down the back stairway," Moody said. These stairs led to the old Arcade Court, and from there the two men could see the reflection of the fire, now about a half mile away on the west side of the city.

"I must get home!" Moody said. Sankey agreed, but decided he would go to the river where the fire was raging. The two parted, neither knowing it would be two months before they saw each other again.

When Sankey got to where the fire was, he could hardly believe his eyes. A whole block of small wooden buildings was burning!

"Help us tear down these fences!" a man shouted at him. "We want to keep the fire from spreading!"

Sankey went to work helping tear down the wooden fences, hoping to make a firebreak, but two months of drought had made Chicago into a tinderbox.

To make matters worse, the wind came up to almost hurricane force, and embers from the falling buildings were picked up and carried to the roofs of other houses, which were soon in flames, too. The fire spread from block to block, sometimes making a wall of fire twenty to thirty feet high. The light could be seen, it was later reported, for hundreds of miles across the prairies. It seemed the whole city was doomed.

Sankey gave up trying to stop the fire, and hurried back to Farwell Hall where he had been living as well as working. As he ran, he shook hot embers off his coat to keep the fire from burning him.

Quickly Sankey put some of his belongings close to his office door while he went to find someone to carry them to safety. It was now between one and two in the morning, and there was no carriage, cart, or wagon anywhere. Sankey hefted the things himself and headed for Lake Michigan, a half mile away.

Struggling with his two large traveling bags, Sankey was making tortuously slow progress. When he got as far as the Palmer House, then under construction, he had an idea.

"I'll hide my bags in the cellar and come back for them later," he thought.

Walking carefully down a plank that went into the cellar, Sankey put his bags in the darkest corner he could find.

As he came out, he could see people hanging out the windows to see the fire, but no one appeared to take it seriously or personally. It was more like watching a horrible play from the safety of the audience.

"Get out!" Sankey screamed at them. "The city's on fire! Save what you can!"

The people paid no attention; some even laughed. It made Sankey remember the Bible story of Sodom and Gomorrah and wonder if it may have looked a lot like this.

With his bags in the cellar of the Palmer House, Sankey hurried back to Farwell for another load of his things, then started directly for the lake. The glare from the fire lighted the streets for him.

Sankey decided to leave this load on the front

steps of a rich-looking house and then went back to his room for still another load. When he got back to the house where he had left his things on the front steps, they were already covered by what others had left there. He never saw those belongings again.

Now the air was filled with flying sparks, making Sankey think briefly of a spring snowstorm. People were running this way and that, many with no idea of where they were going.

As Sankey walked, two men came past carrying a sick man on a stretcher. The sick man, arguing that the city was not in danger (and perhaps tired of being bumped along), ordered the two men to put him down.

"I'll hire you!" Sankey said to them, quickly stepping in to take advantage of this help.

The men helped him carry his things to the edge of the lake. Then they looked toward the south, and gasped. "The fire's coming right at where we live!" They dropped the rest of Sankey's belongings and took off, not even stopping to be paid.

Sankey estimated he would have time to go back to the Palmer House for the bags he had stashed there, although he doubted if they would still be there. But they were, and he brought them to the water's edge, too. His plan was to walk into the lake to wait it out if the fire came too close.

By now Sankey was exhausted, and his throat ached for a drink of water. The lake water near the shore was not safe to drink, so he turned back, stopping at a house to ask for water.

"There's a faucet in back," he was told. "Take all you want."

Eagerly Sankey turned on the faucet, but only air rushed out. It was his first clue that the city water works was a fire victim, too. A few minutes later, a loud explosion shook the city . . . the gas works had blown up. Now Chicago had no water, no lights in the houses, and the city was in flames.

The only thing left to do, it seemed to Sankey, was to go back to the lake and the belongings he had left there. Once there, he wrapped himself in his overcoat and lay down behind one of the large trunks he had saved.

Just an hour after he went to sleep, he was awakened by the roar of the fire engines coming closer. The wind was still high, and now waves were lapping at his feet. The sun, rising over the lake, looked like another big ball of fire to him.

"I have to have water!" Sankey staggered along the shore until he came across some small rowboats, usually for rent to people to enjoy boating on the lake.

"Sure, you can have one," the owner said. "There's fresh water out in the lake." Then, looking at the white-capped waves, "If you can handle the boat."

Sankey rowed the boat back to where he'd left his things, loaded them into the boat, and rowed out to where the water was safe to drink. After drinking his fill, he tied the boat to timbers that were being used to put up a new breakwater, climbed out of the boat and onto the pile of lumber, and watched the destruction of the city behind him.

The city was going fast. Every few minutes there was a loud explosion. Later Sankey learned that these were buildings being blown up on orders of General Sheridan who was in Chicago at the time. The idea was to try to form a barrier against the fire and keep it from spreading to the south.

Looters were starting to get into action now. Sankey saw thieves carrying bales of silks and satins they had taken from burning stores, and walking along the railroad tracks. They didn't know that at one point they would run into fire insurance agents who were waiting for them!

At the end of the day the city was still burning. Sankey decided it was time to go back to land, but when he jumped into his boat, it floated free of the timbers he had tied it to.

The constant up-and-down motion of the boat on the waves had sawed the rope almost in two, and Sankey's sudden weight had finished the job.

Now Ira was in danger again, but from water, not fire, this time. Being out on the lake, where the boat seemed to be drifting, was dangerous. In the strong wind, and with the high waves, the little boat could easily overturn in the choppy water. It was already being swamped with the waves that swept over it.

Sankey worked and prayed—finally managing to get the boat under control—and headed back for shore.

It was a tired song leader who finally stepped back onto land, knowing it was God and not his own skill or strength that had saved him from death.

Again on land, Sankey looked for someone to carry his things. For ten dollars, a greatly inflated price, he found a man with a wagon to take him and his goods to the unburned end of the Fort Wayne and Chicago Railroad.

At the station, Sankey checked his things through to home, got a decent meal at a restaurant, and then walked back to the burnt area of the city.

Farwell Hall was gone, as was the Illinois Street Church. Later Sankey would find out that Moody's house had also burned, although the family escaped.

Moody often said, "All I saved was my Bible, my family, and my reputation."

The city's paved streets were covered with hot bricks and long coils of burned and twisted telegraph wires. Sankey made his way slowly and sadly through the hot streets to the railroad and got on board a train to go home to New Castle.

As he left the city, Sankey could see that parts of it were still burning, and it looked to him as though the whole country were on fire. He could see banks of flames in all directions, and the air was filled with suffocating smoke.

Sankey was sure his work in Chicago with Moody was finished—lost along with the city.

Chapter

4

Moving the British Isles for Christ

ONCE AGAIN, Ira had not given Moody enough credit for his enthusiasm for preaching and building a new church. Moody started right away to raise money for a "tabernacle" in Chicago.

Moody's methods and appeals included everyone. He asked rich men like John Wanamaker, the Philadelphia department store owner, for a large sum, but he was also aware of the power of many small gifts. Children in hundreds of Sunday school classes each gave a nickel to buy a brick to put in the new building.

Sankey soon heard from Moody, urging him to come to Chicago to work with him in the new church and program.

"The Tabernacle will be dedicated the day before Christmas," Moody told him.

We don't know what Ira was expecting when he first saw the new "tabernacle," but the sight must have been a little disappointing. Instead of a large, beautiful building, the church was more like a big barn with a flat roof.

"We thought we'd have to make it smaller," Moody said excitedly, "but we got enough money to almost double that size. It's all of 75 feet by 109 feet now. The men did the work themselves, working at night and in their spare time after work."

Inside, the Tabernacle had rough boards, but more than 1,000 people, young and old, came to the dedication.

Sankey and Moody slept in a little classroom in a corner of their barn-like church. It was not a comfortable place to live and sleep. The winter winds blew off the prairies and came through the big cracks, bringing both snow and cold. This was especially hard on Ira, who all his life had hated drafts.

Ira could easily see the problems and weaknesses of this tabernacle, and Moody agreed. He was determined to build a church that would be permanent, and within a year it was started. By the spring of 1873, the congregation was meeting on its first floor.

"It's only a temporary roof," Moody told everyone, "until we get enough money to build higher. I am not going into debt for that . . . I saw what happened to the Y, my church, and my home in the big fire. I won't risk that."

Ira helped with the running of the tabernacle along with singing and playing at the many meetings, but he could see that Moody was getting restless. He wanted to go back to Great Britain where he had been three times before. And he wanted a song leader to go with him.

At first Ira was not even considered for the trip. He was to stay in Chicago and keep the work going at the tabernacle. Instead, Moody asked another man to go with him, and when he was turned down, asked a second man. He, too, had already made other plans that he felt could not be changed.

Now Moody turned to Ira. "You've often proposed that we should go out evangelizing together. Go with me to England."

"I don't see how I can," Ira replied. "I'm already booked to do a singing tour of the West Coast with someone else. And what about the work here in Chicago?"

"The British call is important enough for me to take you from that work here for a few months, at least."

Ira was torn once again. Should he go with Moody, whom he often called "D.L.," or should he keep the commitment he had already made with another singer for a tour? He decided to ask a trusted friend's advice.

The friend was definite. "Go with Mr. Moody. Two singers on a tour together might clash."

Moody promised Ira a salary of $1200 for the trip, but the two had only a vague idea of where to start.

"We plan to go north," Ira told his family. "We

would like to spend three months in northern England and Scotland, preaching, then come back to America."

On June 7, 1873, Ira and Fanny, along with Moody and his family, sailed for Liverpool, England, on the steamship *City of Paris*. They had their tickets, but only about $450 to live on. The men didn't worry much about that, however, because they knew that three men in England had promised to help them with money, although the money had not yet come.

The trip across the Atlantic took ten days. For Ira and Fanny it was a peaceful, relaxing time. Moody was not as fortunate: he was seasick most of the trip and had to stay in his cabin.

Ira spent much of the voyage going over the poems in his special scrapbook. Next to his Bible, Ira's scrapbook was his most important tool in his work for the Lord. In it he pasted poems and other clippings cut from newspapers and Christian publications. He planned to set some of them to music, making them into hymns. On the trip to England, he wrote the music to the refrain of "Only Trust Him."

When the *City of Paris* docked at Queenstown, Ireland, to pick up mail, Moody and Sankey got bad news. All three of the men who had promised to sponsor them had died! They now had no funds and could not expect any.

The two families did have relatives in the London area, and a few friends, but this hardly seemed like enough to keep them in England—or even get them back to the United States.

"God seems to have closed the doors, Sankey," Moody said. "We will not open any ourselves. If He opens a door, we will go in; otherwise, we will return to America."

Saddened and discouraged, the men and their families stayed on the ship until they got to Liverpool. There in the hotel, Moody began rummaging through his pockets. Suddenly he pulled out a letter he had received just before they left New York.

"I forgot all about this," he said, surprised.

The letter was from the YMCA secretary in York, England. He had written that if Moody and Sankey ever came to England, he hoped they would come to York to hold meetings.

"The door is only ajar," Moody told his song leader, "but we will consider this letter as God's hand leading us to York, and we will go there."

Leaving their families with relatives, the two men went on to York. When they got there they found that everyone considered this a bad time to start religious meetings.

"It's summer and a great many people are on holiday at the beach," they were told. "Holiday," as the men knew, was the English way of saying "vacation."

This news did not stop the two evangelists from going ahead and planning their meetings.

Ira wrote an ad for the newspaper: "D.L. Moody of Chicago will preach, and Ira D. Sankey of Chicago will sing, at 7 o'clock p.m. tomorrow, and each succeeding evening for a week, in the Independent Chapel. All are welcome." Then he added two words that may have helped some people make up their minds to come: "No collection!"

That first night fewer than 50 people showed up, most apparently coming out of curiosity to see the "Yankees" and the "tricks" they might have. The audience was introduced that night to a new and strange music that Ira had called "gospel songs."

One reason for the small crowd was the coolness of the local pastors. They were not enthused about letting these strangers and their type of service be held in their churches. There was also a fear that somehow these men would lure the "flock" away from the established church—and them.

Despite the less than rousing reception at the first meeting, it did give the two zealous men a chance to announce a noon prayer meeting the next day. It was that prayer meeting that would turn the tide in Moody and Sankey's favor.

Although only six came to the prayer meeting that noon in a dingy room at the YMCA building, one of them was a pastor who had been convinced by Moody that he needed to get closer to the Lord.

"That was the rod in God's hand that smote the rock in the desert of doubt and unbelief at York," Ira was to say later.

By Sunday there was a crowd of a thousand, and from then on the only problem for Moody and Sankey was being sure that everyone who wanted to come had a place to sit!

The partners in evangelism stayed five weeks in York, then headed north to Sunderland.

Ira had been spending a lot of his time when not in the meetings sitting at his harmonium and "singing the gospel," as he called it, with the windows wide open. One person would stop to listen, then another, until there would be a crowd standing under the window. Many listening heard the gospel for the first time this way.

A problem arose about the songs Ira was singing at the meetings. "So few of your solos are in our hymnals," went the complaint. Most churches sang the Psalms and only a few other hymns; Ira's songs were new to them, even though they liked them.

At first Ira tried lending out his own scrapbook, but he soon learned that it was not always returned to him in time for the services. That, of course, was a real problem!

Ira decided to have the words of some of the hymns printed on cards. But as soon as the congregation found out these were free, they made a dash for the platform and took them all. It was obvious to Ira that he could not afford to keep doing this!

His next idea was to ask the publishers of the hymnal they were using in the services to add some of the Sankey tunes in the back, but this suggestion was turned down.

When the men were in Sunderland, Ira mentioned these bad experiences to a publisher friend. The friend offered to take some of Ira's songs to

London and publish them in a small paperback pamphlet. Immediately Ira cut 23 pieces from his scrapbook, rolled them up, and wrote on them "Sacred Songs and Solos, sung by Ira D. Sankey at the meetings of Mr. Moody of Chicago."

In two weeks Ira had 500 copies of the booklet. They sold for six pence each, and before the first day of using them was over, they were all gone. More copies were sent, and these soon sold out, too. They were the start of a book which, even though it contained the words only, grew to be a thick volume of 1200 pieces. The book was usually just called "Sankey's," and people ordered it by that name.

Moody and Sankey took no profits from the sale of this and other songbooks. They used the money to help build Moody's church in Chicago and, later, some schools. Ira also gave funds for a new YMCA building in New Castle, Pennsylvania.

Another first at Sunderland was Ira's use of the small pump organ called the "harmonium." He was said to tower over this small instrument and to sway with the music as he played and sang. The tunes, like the words, were catchy—completely different from the slow, formal music the people were used to in their churches. The tunes were quickly picked up by the people.

One meeting in Sunderland was especially dramatic. Ira was singing "Come Home, O Prodigal," when there was a loud cry: "O Father, will you forgive me?" A young man rushed down the middle aisle to where his father was sitting and threw his arms around his neck, begging him for forgiveness. The father stood up. "My boy, I forgive everything. Come now, let us go to the vestry and ask God to forgive us both, as I have forgiven you."

That night hundreds of people jammed the adjoining room after the service for prayer and counseling.

The next stop for the Moody and Sankey team was in Newcastle where Ira organized the first choir for their meetings.

Not everything was solemn, though. In one small town, the organ, borrowed for the service, did well until the end of the meeting. With Moody in one room, speaking to those who wanted to know more about committing to the Lord, Ira was in another room, leading a prayer service. Suddenly the organ began, on its own, to give out horrible sounds. Ira rushed to try to stop the noise, but could not. The prayer meeting came to an abrupt end.

After spending some time in England, the men went to Scotland. Here the organ was called "kist o'whistles," and the churches were set against "human hymns." At the first meeting in Edinburgh Moody had a bad cold, so Ira was put in charge of the meeting, working with a visiting preacher.

Ira won the people over to his songs by starting with a part of the 100th Psalm, which everyone knew, then going into his own songs.

The men also went to Glasgow. On the train on the way back to Edinburgh, Ira began to read the small weekly paper he had bought for a penny just before getting on the train. There was no news of America, as he had hoped, but he found a poem in a corner of one page. It was by an Elizabeth C. Clephane, and was called "The Ninety and Nine," based on the parable of Jesus about the Good Shepherd. Ira loved it and was excited, thinking it would make a great hymn if he added music.

"Moody, listen to this!" Ira read his friend the poem, but Moody was not impressed. Ira cut out the poem anyway and put it in his scrapbook.

At a meeting the next day, Moody preached on "The Good Shepherd," and when he was finished, turned to Ira and asked him to sing "something appropriate."

Immediately Ira thought of the 23rd Psalm, but they had sung it already. Then he seemed to hear a voice telling him to "sing the hymn you found on the train." With no music to go with the words, Ira felt this would be impossible. But the urging came again. Praying God would help him sing it, Ira put the poem on the organ, struck the key of A-flat, and began to sing. The tune came to him note by note, and it has never been changed!

When the meeting was over, Moody rushed to Ira. "Where did you get that song? It's beautiful!" His eyes were wet.

Ira gently told him it was the poem that had not impressed him on the train!

Later, Ira met the poet's sister, who thanked him for putting music to the poem. Elizabeth had died without ever knowing that her words would lead people around the world to the Lord—without having read any of the many letters Ira got from them.

After Scotland came Ireland, where there was no objection to "Sankey tunes," and then came London again.

By now the success of the meetings had made Moody and Sankey household names in Britain, and the crowds coming to hear them preach and sing were large.

Just as happens with famous people today, though, jokes and parodies of Sankey's hymns began to be used by comedians for laughs. But the people didn't laugh. At one show in London, when a comedian changed the words of a hymn, he was hissed off the stage.

At a circus in another town, one clown said to another, "I am rather Moody tonight; how do you feel?"

His partner answered, "I feel rather Sankeymonious."

At this the audience not only hissed, they stood up and sang "Hold the Fort"—one of Ira's tunes.

The British tour came to an end when the partners sailed for home on August 3, 1875, on the ship *Spain*. The crowd on the shore sang their hymns until the ship was out of sight.

Used by permission, The Billy Graham Center Museum

The revivalists, Moody and Sankey, opening a service in Brooklyn, New York.

Chapter

5

Home to America

WHEN MOODY and Sankey got back to the United States in August 1875, they found the news of their work and success in Britain had preceded them to this country. They were treated almost like heroes, and towns and cities across the country wanted them to come. They could choose the places they wanted to visit, and immediately they began planning tours that, it turned out, would last for several years.

Their first stop was Northfield, Massachusetts, Moody's hometown. From there they went to Brooklyn, where Ira organized a choir of 250 local singers to help him with the musical part of the services. Although they were using a big building for their meetings, they had to turn people away.

The setup for the American revivals was similar to what Moody and Sankey had worked out during their English tours. They usually arrived a day or so early to check out the physical arrangements. That extra day gave Ira a chance to rehearse at least once with his local choir, which usually had singers from more than one church in it. The early visit also gave them time to get to know the local workers and make sure that everything would go smoothly.

A huge platform, large enough to hold not only the big choir but several hundred local important people, was built at the front of the hall. Of course it took a special invitation to sit on the platform. These invitations were sent, not by Moody and Sankey, but by the ministers of the city that had invited the evangelists. Naturally, the local ministers and leading businessmen occupied these seats, and the people in the audience often spent a lot of time checking to see just who had made it to these prized seats in front.

Moody spoke from a dais, or pulpit, with a rail around it and raised a foot or so above the rest of the platform. Ira always put himself and his organ close by, often just next to Moody's right hand. This let both men see the audience and the audience see both of them.

Just below the platform were desks for the reporters. Sometimes a reporter would hand Ira a slip of paper—a request for a specific hymn.

Usually the services were held in big buildings that had been used as warehouses or railroad depots, or in barnlike buildings built especially for Moody and Sankey. These buildings were hard to beautify, although sometimes banners with Bible verses or messages were strung around the big room.

Because the setting was so informal, the services, too, tended to be a lot more lively than the usual Sunday morning services most people were used to.

A half hour of congregational singing started every large meeting. Ira used this time to teach the congregation new tunes. It also helped set the stage for the rest of the meeting and muffled the noise and confusion of latecomers looking for seats!

Every service had an "inquiry room," a special room for prayer and consultation after the service. People came to the inquiry room to learn more about becoming Christians, and to talk to Moody and Sankey and the ministers helping them.

One night in Brooklyn, Ira was talking to a young man in the inquiry room. "Do you want to accept Christ as your Savior?" Ira asked. It was the first question he always asked, since most people coming to the room were close to making such a decision.

"Jesus will not accept me." The young man went on to tell Ira how he had talked against Jesus and His followers around the world. "He will not forgive me," he ended.

"Do you want Him to?" Ira asked.

"I don't even know why I'm here!" the young man replied. "Some power I don't understand has been working on me for two days and I'm despondent."

Silently Ira prayed that he would know how to deal with this man, and not make any mistakes.

"What you need tonight, my dear friend," Ira said, "is Christ. He will dispel your gloom and sorrow."

"But I have fought Him all my life, and I thought I was right!"

"Did you have peace when you were speaking against Christ?" Ira asked.

"No." The young man then told Ira about coming home on a ship when a storm came up, driving them toward the rocks. "I got down on my knees and prayed to God to save us. The storm died, and with it my prayers. As soon as we were safe, I went back to denying there was a God."

"Let that go!" Ira ordered. "What brought you here tonight?"

"I don't know. About a year ago my mother in Scotland wrote, asking me to promise to go to services if Moody and Sankey ever came near. I promised, and I came two nights, and haven't had any rest since! I decided to come one more time and here I am!"

"It's the answer to your mother's prayers," Ira said. "She may be praying for you right now. Don't delay. Yield to Christ and He will receive you."

The man bowed his head and, after a long time, finally took Ira's hand and said, "By the grace of God, I take Jesus Christ as my Savior now!"

Ira told the young man to write to his mother, and when the man came back a few nights later he reported that he had sent a simple cable to his mother: "I have found Jesus."

"Praise the Lord!" Ira said.

The man smiled. "That's just what my mother

cabled back to me."

There were many such experiences in the inquiry room in every city, but there were other interesting experiences, too.

In Philadelphia the team were guests of John Wanamaker, the owner of "The Largest Clothing Store in America." Wanamaker had bought the freight depot that covered a city block, paying $500,000. Then he spent $35,000 to make it into a temporary tabernacle. It may have been one of the nicest halls the men had. In addition, Wanamaker got many of his clerks to help as ushers or choir members.

There were 11,000 chairs in rows, and red, white and blue bunting everywhere. This was the year of America's 100th birthday, and the big Centennial Exposition was planned for the city.

President Grant came to Philadelphia while Moody and Sankey were there to check on the Exposition's preparations. Naturally he and all his staff were invited to sit on the platform of a Moody and Sankey meeting! That way the whole audience got to see him as well as the evangelists.

Later, when Moody and Sankey had left for the next city on their schedule, the furnishings of the tabernacle were auctioned off. The chair President Grant had sat in sold for $25; Moody's and Sankey's chairs each brought $55!

Revivals were also held in New York City and Chicago. At one of the Chicago meetings Moody spotted an usher whose looks he didn't like. Since all the ushers were provided by the area churches, Moody asked the chairman of the committee who the man was.

"I don't know, but I'll find out." A few minutes later the chairman was back. "His name is Charles Guiteau," he reported.

The name meant nothing to Moody; no one had any idea that this same Guiteau would be the one who later shot President Garfield.

In every city people came to the inquiry rooms and professed their faith in Christ. In addition to the work in the cities, Moody and Sankey were also invited to the campuses of both Princeton and Yale universities to talk and sing with the students there. Again, they helped many come to Christ.

But D.L. and Ira were not all seriousness. Both liked a good joke—especially when it was on the other one!

One time, when Ira's wife, Fanny, was with them, Ira announced he was going to take a bath.

Moody answered, "I thought you only took a bath once a year."

"And your time's just about up," Fanny laughed.

Ira took the teasing well. "Fanny, it's bad enough to have Moody down on me without you taking his part."

Back in Boston, the meetings lasted six months, with an average of three meetings a day. There were also special meetings for men, women, and even children.

Although Ira was used to criticism about his singing, and even people making fun of him, one newspaper writer in Boston was especially hard on him. In one of his columns the man wrote a parody of the refrain of "Hold the Fort, for I Am Coming." His version was: Hold the forks, the knives are coming . . . The plates are on the way . . . Shout the chorus to your neighbor . . . Sling the hash this way."

Another time, this critic drew a cartoon figure of Ira at his organ. He made a big mistake, though, when he tried to make fun of him by showing tears running down his face. Anyone who had been at a Moody and Sankey meeting knew that was just how intense Ira was about his singing for the Lord.

These things bothered Ira, but since people did not seem to be turned off by them, the meetings went on, with no letup in attendance.

Ira, a better looking man than Moody, was always dressed neatly and precisely. He brought a touch of glamour to the meetings—a masculine appeal that the women all noticed. After one Brooklyn meeting, Ira was surrounded by a "fluttering group of female admirers," all wanting to talk to him. He laughed and gently pushed them aside, saying in a loud voice, "Any who wish to speak with me concerning their souls will please step into the chapel. I have no time for anything else."

In other cities too, it was often Ira, not Mr. Moody, who was hounded by the autograph seekers.

In Hartford, Connecticut, several famous people came to the meetings. One was Mark Twain, author of the popular *Tom Sawyer* and *Huckleberry Finn* books. Another was P.T. Barnum, owner of the famous circus. After the meeting, Barnum went to the inquiry room to speak to Ira.

"Mr. Sankey, you go on singing 'The Ninety and Nine,' and when you get that lost sheep in the fold we will all be saved."

In Chattanooga, Tennessee, the evangelistic team ran into the race problem. Racial segregation was openly practiced in the South; less openly in the North. Now the two evangelists found their meetings were being boycotted by the city's African Americans because none of their ministers had been invited to sit on the platform with the white pastors.

"We'll have a special meeting just for the colored," Moody decided, using the term then popular for African Americans.

The meeting was announced, but when Ira got to the building that night, it was almost empty, although the men had expected a big crowd.

Moody was not discouraged. He personally went out into the street to invite hundreds of African Americans to the meeting. With his personal invitation, they came, and nothing more was said about boycotting the meetings.

Another six-month campaign was held in St. Louis. One night Ira approached a man leaving the building. "Are you a Christian?" Ira asked.

"No," he was told, "I'm a Missourian!"

We don't know what Ira answered to that!

Going across the country, Moody and Sankey

refused to travel on Sunday. They would stop and stay over wherever they were so they could worship on the Lord's Day. This led, one time, to their having their "day of rest" in Salt Lake City, the headquarters of the Mormon church. The evangelists were invited to preach and sing at both the Presbyterian and Methodist churches in the city, and were welcomed so warmly that they ended up staying two weeks instead of one day!

Once, traveling on a train from Chicago to New York City, Ira sat beside a stranger. After they had discussed the weather and moved on to current events, the man said he had never heard this Moody and Sankey team.

"I have, many times!" Ira said, but did not tell the man who he was. "They're just common folks like you and me."

"Well, I wish I could have heard Sankey sing 'The Ninety and Nine' before he died," the man said longingly.

"But Sankey isn't dead!" Ira said. "Where did you hear that?"

"It was in the newspaper!" That seemed to be proof positive for him!

By this time the train was getting close to the man's station, so Ira told him who he was, and that he could see he was still very much alive, despite what the paper had said.

Ira expected the stranger to laugh and be glad the gospel singer was not dead. Instead, the man glared at him. "You can't fool me! Sankey is dead!"

He grabbed his bag and left, never knowing that he had been talking to the very man he had wanted to hear sing.

By now the names "Moody" and "Sankey" were being talked about everywhere, and the two were always said together in the same breath! Many people almost began to think of them as just one man, not two individuals!

At a church in Norfolk, the minister asked Moody to let him say something before the meeting began. "This is Mr. Moody," he told the congregation, nodding toward Moody. "And the man at the organ is Mr. Sankey. They are not the same person!"

Ira always knew Moody was the leader of their duo, but he also realized that his "singing the gospel" was just as important as Moody's preaching in bringing people to Jesus. Ira always prayed for souls before singing, and he knew well that many people would remember the words of the songs—and sing them over and over—but forget most of the sermon they had heard.

The gospel songs Ira wrote were simple, catchy tunes, and he always picked ones for the service that fit in with Moody's theme of the night. He also used songs with a chorus that the audience could easily pick up after a verse or two. Using the chorus for the audience to sing, and the verses for himself or the choir, Ira was able to "play" them against each other, letting everyone in the congregation be part of the service.

Because Ira wrote such simple, singable tunes, people could remember them, and often left the meetings humming them. The words always fit the music, usually giving information from God's Word and always trying to create a mood for admitting sin and looking to Jesus for salvation.

Ira once told a reporter, "You can't do it all with music alone; you've got to make them hear every word and see every picture. . . . Then you'll get that silence of death, that quiet before God." To do this, Ira sang each verse differently, matching his tone with the words, and trying very hard to sing the words precisely and clearly, so no one would miss hearing them.

In England, Ira had begun to introduce each of his solos with a short "sermonette" that told about how someone had been saved through hearing this particular gospel hymn, or how it had come to be written. Over the years, he sang many gospel songs that were not his own, and it gave the American audiences more than just a song to think about.

Although most of Ira's tunes being simple and easy to remember were good, in Boston—and a few other places as well—some people made quite different use of his music than he had intended. The songs had a lot of the popular-music form of the times, so the words were easily changed to the secular, yet still sung to the same Sankey tunes.

In the presidential race of 1877, "Hold the Fort" was secularized again. This time it was changed to "Hold the Fort for Hayes and Wheeler." (And they were elected!)

In Chicago, couples waltzed to a jazzy form of "Almost Persuaded." This was not what Ira had wanted for his tunes, but fortunately he apparently never heard of this last use of his music.

For the next few years Moody and Sankey visited cities in the United States, Canada and Mexico. But Great Britain was calling them again.

Chapter

6

Back to Britain

ALL OVER AMERICA the Moody and Sankey meetings had been successful. Huge crowds had come, and many people had accepted Christ in the inquiry rooms after the meetings.

Now, in 1879, invitations were coming in from Great Britain to make a second trip there. One invitation, signed by ministers and lay people, was 150 yards long!

The two men talked it over. It seemed like an opportune time for them to leave America and revisit some of the places they had worked in six years before. And add some new cities to their schedule as well.

The plans for these meetings were much like the ones they had followed on their last visit to Great Britain. Only this time there was no problem getting cities to invite them to come, or crowds to fill the halls wanting to hear Ira sing his gospel songs as he accompanied himself on the organ.

When Ira had gone to Glasgow, Scotland, in 1874, one newspaper writer had described his songs as "so new, so peculiar," that "careful inquiry" into the legitimacy of his efforts was necessary! The idea of preaching the gospel through music and "human hymns" was suspicious.

Also on the first visit, Ira's "kist o'whistles" was suspect. Only a few churches had organs, and then mostly for display. Those against church organs claimed there was "a devil in every pipe." But the people had accepted Ira's small harmonium and now no one thought about it when he played it. His songs were easy to learn and eagerly sung by the people, and the local ministers did not have to be convinced that inviting Moody and Sankey to their town would be good for their churches!

Wherever the two went they met people who had become Christians during the team's first tour of the country. There had been questions about whether or not such "conversions" would stick, but these people proved they had. They were active in their churches and speaking for the Lord whenever possible.

At one point someone asked Moody if he kept records of the number of conversions at his meetings. "Records! Why, they are only kept in Heaven!" That summed up the way both men felt about the work they were doing. It was for God, not themselves!

Ira felt strongly that while he was singing the

gospel, he was also preparing the people for Moody's message.

By the time the men got to Scotland they had added something more to their already full schedule. They now were holding Sunday morning meetings for children. Brought by parents and grandparents, the children would crowd around the men. Ira and his organ got a lot of special attention from the youngsters who were curious about how it worked.

About this time Ira became aware of how many hymns he had written, and decided it was time to follow a custom of the day among gospel song writers. He would use a pen name for some of his work.

"That way it will keep from looking like I'm doing too much under my own name," Ira thought. He decided on the pen name "Rian A. Dykes." This may seem like a strange name to come up with. But when you rearrange the letters of the pen name, they can spell "Ira D. Sankey."

Ira used his pen name not only on some of his music, but also in writing home to his family. Actually, the name was so convincing that it was many years before people outside his family and close friends knew that "Rian" was really "Ira."

In Liverpool, the people with things to sell wanted to get in on Moody and Sankey's popularity and the big crowds that came to their meetings. They took full advantage of the situation.

Although booksellers were not allowed in the building itself, there was nothing to stop them from setting up booths right outside, where the people had to pass them to get into the meetings. You could buy a lot of different things at these booths, making it seem more like a carnival than the entrance to a religious meeting. There were knickknacks, cheap food (and its odors!), drawings of the two men, pamphlets, and hymn books.

There were even small statues of the men, some ten inches high and others eighteen inches tall. Many of the homes in Great Britain would keep the pair sitting on the mantle over the fireplace for years, reminding them of their visit to hear the gospel in song and sermon.

Any photos of the men were crude. One photographer offered the two men about $5,000 if they would let him take their picture and copyright it. They turned him down, and later he wrote to *The Times* to let everyone know the men were not out to make money from their popularity.

In London they tried something new. Instead of using buildings already in place, they had two portable tabernacles constructed. Each would seat 5,000 people. These were moved around the city; the one not being used at the time for meetings was moved to the next location.

Many times one of these tabernacles was taken to the more crowded, poorer parts of the city so everyone could hear the message of Christ.

At one of these Moody and Sankey meetings a young medical student, on his way home from seeing a patient, stopped in. He was impressed by both men, went to a meeting later held in conjunction with Moody and Sankey, and there accepted the Lord.

Years later, Sir Wilfred Grenfell became famous as a medical missionary to Labrador.

As Moody and Sankey traveled around the country, rumors kept cropping up about their personal finances, especially from the sale of so many of the songbooks they had brought out. These were used in all the services, and almost everyone who came to a meeting bought a songbook for himself.

"They just have those services to sell the books," some people began to say. The truth was just the opposite. The profits from the book sales would have made both men rich, but neither took a penny for himself.

Moody used book money to begin three schools. One, for girls, was at Northfield, near his home. Here he also started a yearly evangelistic conference that brought evangelists together. Five miles away, he established a school for boys. Later on, these two schools became one, known as Northfield Schools.

Another school became the Moody Bible Institute of today—in Chicago. There, at Ira's insistence, a music program was included.

For his part, Ira built and furnished a YMCA building for New Castle that cost $43,000. The library in the new building had about 3,000 books, almost all donated by him. At the time it was considered one of the best collections in the country. When the building was dedicated, Ira was there to play the organ for the group singing.

Neither did Ira forget the church where he had first begun to sing and had been the Sunday school superintendent. He gave the First Methodist Church a lot in New Castle on which to build a new church.

Ira also gave a hall to each of the schools Moody had established in Massachusetts.

But in Great Britain the long hours of work were taking their toll on everyone involved with planning and leading the meetings. It was especially hard on Ira. There were meetings at least two times a day, and often four or five.

Singing so often, without a microphone or any way to amplify his voice, Ira's voice was starting to be affected. Although the acoustics were better during this trip, there still was a degree of strain.

In addition to having problems with his voice, Ira's nerves were also starting to get worn from all the pressure of so much singing. He was suffering, too, from painful neuralgia. There was only one answer.

"I will have to quit the tour before our London meetings are over," he told Moody sadly. "If I am to save my voice, I must go back to America."

Back in the States, Ira and Fanny bought a house in Brooklyn, New York. There they would live during the winters when Ira was not with Moody. The summers they spent mostly at Northfield, helping with the conferences there. Ira and Fanny loved their home, and filled it with mementos and gifts from his many tours.

Later, in 1891, Moody and Sankey made a third

trip to Great Britain, but this one was different from the first two. They planned to cover 99 towns in 90 days! And hold at least three meetings in each place!

Again, Ira had to leave early and come back to America to rest. Moody, whose energy had once seemed without limit, was also feeling the strain. He was finally persuaded by his friends to go to a doctor about a cold that hung on.

"You have an irregular heartbeat, Mr. Moody," the doctor told him. "You must slow up."

But Moody could not do that. When he came back to America, he and Ira planned a big campaign at the World's Columbian Exposition, in Chicago, that would be open from May through October, 1893. The big fair commemorated the 400th anniversary of Columbus and his ships landing in the New World.

"Why is it going to be a year late?" people wondered. "Columbus landed in 1492, not 1493!"

The answer was simple. Chicago had not been able to get ready for the big celebration in time to make the 1892 date!

"Why Chicago at all?" was another question. "Columbus was never near it!" Many cities bigger and richer than Chicago had wanted the Exposition to come to their town. The final decision was up to Congress.

"They picked Chicago because the businessmen there had the money," was one opinion.

The real reason for choosing Chicago was that it had a park big enough for the Exposition right along Lake Michigan. And large ships could dock there.

Moody saw the Exposition as the opportunity of the century to reach people for Christ. There would be all of the Chicago area people, plus probably millions coming from all over the world for the big celebration.

There was one big problem for the evangelists: the fair was open on Sundays. In fact, that was usually the biggest day of the week for visitors and money.

It might have been possible to prosecute the fair legally to make them close on the Lord's Day, but Moody took a different route. He would fight the fair's Sunday opening with religious services.

Local churches, volunteers, and students from the Moody Bible Institute began preaching. In addition, Moody brought the best preachers from other countries to Chicago to preach to visitors in their own languages.

It worked. More people came to hear Moody and Sankey and the other preachers than went to the fair, and the fair finally gave up and closed on Sundays.

Then the Forepaugh Circus came to town. For Sunday morning services Moody rented their big tent that held 18,000 people. Then he began to advertise the services. When some ministers objected to advertising religious services, Moody reminded them that businesses advertised, so why shouldn't they.

The first Sunday in the new tent the weather was hot and humid. There was no air conditioning, of course, and the sun beating down on the canvas would surely make it very uncomfortable inside.

"He'll be lucky to get 3,000 to show up," one circus worker said to another as they wiped sweat from their faces.

But by the time the meeting started, the tent was full, even though there was perspiration on every face and the hand-held cardboard fans were moving back and forth at a rapid speed to cool the ladies.

Ira, too, was probably hot and uncomfortable as he sat at the organ. He always wore a coat in the meetings!

The head of the circus was not blind to what was happening on Sunday mornings. And he knew what to do.

"Mr. Moody, would you supply us with an evangelist to go with the circus and handle the Sunday morning crowds?" he asked. To the circus manager's surprise, but not to Ira's, Moody refused.

Once again, though, the strain of so much singing was showing in Ira's voice. He had never had professional voice training; his emphasis in the meetings had been on the words of the hymns and what they meant. He believed that was more effective, but now his voice was worse than ever, even though he was trying to save it as much as he could.

"He flatted frightfully," one young man said to another.

No one could argue with that, least of all Ira who realized what was happening. He decided he was not really helping the meetings any more, and went to talk to Moody. The two men had worked together so closely for so long that they were more like family than partners.

"I'm sorry," Ira told his dear friend, "but I can't go with you through this campaign. My voice has broken. I know it. I thought I could fight it out, but I can't. I've got to quit."

Moody broke down, crying. It would be like losing a part of himself after the 22 years the two had worked together to bring Christ to people around the world. And people wanted Moody and *Sankey*! That was what they had heard and wanted to hear again. But Moody knew his friend was making the right, and very hard, decision.

"Please stay on," Moody asked, "and gradually do less. That way it won't look like you suddenly dropped out of sight, which might make people think we had had an argument and were angry at each other."

Ira agreed, but from then on he appeared less and less often with his old friend, letting other evangelistic singers take his place with Moody. But the two were not finished as partners. They still had a lot of meetings to do as Moody and Sankey.

Chapter

7

More Times with Moody

DESPITE HAVING to leave the latest campaigns early, and having other warning signs that he would have to do more to save his voice, Ira was not yet ready to quit singing for the Lord. Or to quit working with Moody completely. The two were too good a team.

"We'll head south again," the men decided. "And end up in Mexico."

At the meetings on this trip Ira accompanied himself on a traveling organ. It was a simple instrument, built for him by the Estey Company, and given to him several years before. It had been designed specifically for being moved often from city to city. Its sides folded in to make it more compact and easier to transport. (This organ is now in the Lawrence County Historical Society Museum in New Castle, Pennsylvania. Everyone who comes to see it is invited to sit down and play on the same keys Ira did when he sang the gospel to thousands of people.)

In Wilmington, Delaware, Ira was again singing and speaking at six meetings each Sunday. Usually he sang two solos at each one, and once more he could feel that his voice was being strained by so much use.

He wrote to his brother Richard, complaining about the bad weather and the hall where the meetings were being held. It was February, and the weather was cold and damp.

"I do not like sitting in the drafts in this old building," he told Richard.

In those days, "drafts" (cold air blowing right on you) were thought to cause colds and sore throats. These were real threats to singers, and—as we noted earlier—one of the few things Ira feared all his life and tried to stay away from whenever he could. In the old buildings where meetings were usually held, there were many drafty areas in winter.

Ira told Richard that to keep his voice strong for the meetings he would often slip out of the hall when his part was over and go back to where they were staying and rest. Leaving before the meeting was over was not as bad as it sounds; after all, Ira had heard all of Moody's sermons many times by now and could probably have given them himself if asked!

In the same letter, Ira mentioned that he would "cut sticks" for his home in Brooklyn in three more weeks. ("Cut sticks" was popular slang that meant to "make tracks" or to "blast off.")

After holding meetings in both Fort Worth and

El Paso, Texas, they crossed the border into Mexico. The people of Chihuahua heard that the evangelists would be coming through their town on their way farther south. Even though there were no meetings planned for Chihuahua, and the men would be in the city only one day, the people wanted to hear the famous preacher and singer.

Quickly, arrangements were made for special meetings at a local church, and announcements inviting everyone to come were printed. To get the most from the short visit, the people scheduled two meetings, one in the afternoon and one in the evening.

A few days later Moody and Sankey and their team arrived in Mexico City. Once the capital of the Aztec Empire, the city was high above sea level.

The trip here had been hard and dusty, and the men had gone through some of the poorest areas of the country. Ira was now aware that he was about 3,000 miles from home and Fanny.

Now even Moody admitted to being tired, and in Mexico City he stayed away from a special meeting of delegates where he was not the speaker. This was very unusual, but Ira went and closed the meeting by both singing and speaking. It was experiences like this that would be valuable to him later.

The next morning they were on a train at 6:30, headed for the city of Toluca, about 45 miles southwest of Mexico City. Ira was really worried about his voice, and spoke to Moody about it.

"I can't sing so easily here," he told the evangelist. "It's the lack of air at this height. I just don't have the wind."

It was a problem that all visitors faced at that altitude where there is less air pressure. For a singer like Ira, it was especially hard to adjust. He had to sing loudly and with expression, and he needed more air to sing the way he wanted.

Again Ira tried to change his lifestyle and habits, to take it easier and save his strength for singing in the meetings. He walked around the town less than he usually did in new places, trying to keep from getting short of breath. He rested more, too.

Ira was relieved when the Mexico trip was over. He was glad he had gone, of course, but he saw the country as poor and miserable. He was tired of "knocking around," as he put it in another letter to Richard. He was also anxious to get home to his wife and family. He had had only one letter from Fanny while he was in Mexico.

Back in the U.S. again, the men once more faced the problem, especially in the South, of what to do about having African Americans in the meetings.

"We'll set aside one side of the tabernacle for them," Moody decided. It was the way all public gatherings were held then in most of the country—if "Negroes" were allowed in at all.

While both Moody and Sankey wished things were different between the races, they went along with the local customs to prevent any problems with the people in charge of the meetings.

Both men knew that the African Americans were

known for their enthusiastic singing, so they always asked them to sing as a separate group at certain times during each meeting. "That'll show the white people how to sing!" Moody declared.

That summer the men went back to Northfield, as they always did. This was Moody's home and the site of one of the schools he had started. He also scheduled conferences and Bible studies throughout the season.

This part of New England was perfect for relaxing and for quiet Bible studies or religious services. The Connecticut River flowed through the rural area, the hills and forests adding to the beauty.

One of the men who worked with the Moody and Sankey team—who would play a smaller organ while Ira sang—lived in the same cottage with Ira. Years later he remembered going to lunch with the singer one day. After looking at the menu, Ira told the waitress, "Oh, bring me a great deal of everything." He was a big man with a big appetite.

Sometimes Ira had to use psychology to get Moody to go along with what he wanted him to do. At one of these summer services Ira wanted a young lady to play a violin solo. He was pretty sure Moody would not like the idea of using a violin in the service, so he asked the young woman to play a song written by Moody's granddaughter. He himself accompanied her on the organ. The evangelist made no objections!

At another Northfield meeting Ira showed—dramatically but unplanned—his desire to serve others and the Lord every way he could. At the end of a meeting where Moody had been telling the people about a good cause that needed money right away, he turned to Ira. "Mr. Sankey, would you please lead us in prayer for this good work?"

Ira stood up. "Our dear Lord," he began, "we implore thy richest blessings on this worthy cause. May thy children take it to heart . . ."

Suddenly he stopped and looked up. "Wait a minute, folks! Before I go on, Mr. Secretary, put me down for $250, and now, let us pray."

Everyone was stunned by Ira's sudden interruption while praying. They had never heard anyone stop in the middle of a prayer to God to talk to the people in the congregation! But when Ira went on to his "Amen," the money needed was quickly raised!

The incident made such an impression on one man that years later, in 1941, he used it as an example of Christian giving in an article he wrote for *The Sunday School Times*.

That summer Ira was working on a new songbook. His original songbook had grown into a series, with a new one coming out periodically. This newest book would include many of the old hymns everyone knew, along with new ones.

These books contained not only Ira's songs, but gospel songs from many writers. In fact, for Ira the hardest part of editing a new book was having to turn down a friend's song, although he usually managed to get something else by that writer or musician in that book, or a later one.

The friend who had regularly played the organ for him now played it again as Ira carefully followed the words of each hymn being considered for the new book. He took into account the value—or lack of it—of each song and chose only the ones he thought were best.

About this time Ira took on another job. He became president of Biglow & Main, the music publishing company that had brought out so much of his own music.

One of the hymnals he helped with was intended for young people. In it were more than 110 pages of new songs written especially for them.

Summers at Northfield were restful for Ira, even though he took part in many meetings and services. But new experiences were waiting for him, along with some sadness.

Courtesy LCHS

Ira Sankey's cabinet organ which he took with him on his many evangelistic journeys was called a "Kist O'Whistles" in Scotland. The organ is pictured at its permanent location in the Sankey Room at the Lawrence County Historical Society's Clavelli History Center.

Chapter

8

Off to the Holy Land

BUSY WITH MANY different matters, Ira was not giving his body a chance to rest and get strong again.

"You need a rest and change of scene," his doctor told him. "You need to go somewhere where no one knows you, and where you wouldn't be asked to sing so much."

It was hard to think of anywhere in the world where the name Ira D. Sankey was not known. While there were many places around the globe he and Moody had not visited, his *music* had gone there! It was known almost everywhere.

His face, though, would not be so easily recognized. With so few pictures taken of him (and those that were, were not good ones) Ira could go places without being recognized—if he didn't sing.

"I've always wanted to visit the Holy Land," Ira thought. "That could be the answer for me now."

In early 1898, Ira, along with Fanny, his son

Alan, a brother and some friends, sailed from New York City for Alexandria, Egypt. From there they took a train to Cairo, the capital.

The first night they were there, Ira decided to go to the American Mission. When he got there a lecture was going on. The room was crowded with Americans, English and Egyptians, but a two-foot-high partition separated the "natives" from the "foreigners." It may have reminded Ira of the times he and Moody had held meetings in the American South where segregation was the rule.

Thinking how relaxing it would be to sit in a meeting where he didn't have to do anything but listen, Ira slipped into a chair. He was just beginning to feel comfortable and enjoy himself when an American sitting behind him recognized him. "Would you sing for us after the lecture, Mr. Sankey?" he asked.

"If there is an organ or piano," Ira said. He did not want to sing without accompaniment.

There was no organ or piano in the hall, so the man forgot it. Then another missionary, who happened to come from the same part of western Pennsylvania as Ira did, also recognized him.

When she was told he would sing if there was some way to accompany himself, she quickly motioned to four Egyptian soldiers, and they left the hall with her. When they came back they had a small organ which they put on the platform.

When the speaker had finished, Ira was introduced to the audience. He gave a half-hour service of song, both singing solos and having the audience sing with him. Even after Ira thought he had finished, the people asked him to sing more and more.

Ira's hope of not being recognized was now gone. As his group sailed up and down the Nile River, the missionaries along the way often asked him to hold services of song for them when the ship stopped. Ira found it hard to refuse. He was surprised to find that the natives at several places already knew some of the hymns he sang.

The Sankeys and their friends spent forty days in Egypt, seeing all the tourist sights such as the pyramids. At one place Ira had his picture taken with an old Arab who had discovered the mummy of Rameses II.

Once they were in Palestine, they visited all the sites sacred to Christians. Because he had studied the Bible so much, Ira was often able to explain in great detail about the places they visited, and how what had happened there so long ago fit into the Old and New Testaments.

In many of the locations Ira sang a gospel song that was appropriate to that particular spot. But that was not always as easy as it sounds!

In Jerusalem, on his way to the Tower of David, Ira was stopped by a soldier carrying a gun. The man spoke no English, and Ira did not know his language. But with rough gestures, the soldier made it plain that Ira could not go up into the tower without a special permit.

After Ira got that permit from the captain of the

guard, he started up the winding stairway. Close on his heels was another tough-looking soldier, also with a gun.

At the top of the tower, Ira wanted to sing something to honor King David, so he chose the 121st Psalm. As he began to sing, "I will lift up mine eyes unto the hills; from whence cometh my help?" the soldier rushed up, very angry.

Ira kept on singing. Knowing the soldier did not understand a single word, he finished the Psalm. By that time the soldier realized that Ira was not doing anything threatening or dangerous, so he smiled and tipped his hat. Ira smiled and tipped his hat, too.

At Mt. Zion Ira visited a school organized by an English bishop for the children of Jerusalem. The school's principal greeted him eagerly.

"I was in the choir at some of your meetings in London," he told Ira. "Would you sing for our children, please?"

Ira nodded. "But please, have the children sing for me first." To his surprise, the students not only sang their native songs in Arabic, but also some of his own songs.

What affected Ira most, emotionally, was standing with the group on the skull-shaped hill of Calvary. He pictured Jesus hanging there—dying and in great pain—between two thieves to pay for people's sins. To honor his Lord, Ira sang through his tears "On Calvary's Brow My Savior Died."

Everywhere the group went, they heard some of Ira's songs being sung, and when they left the Holy

Land and went to Turkey, Ira was again invited to sing in several Christian churches. That was also true in Rome as they headed for France and home.

During this trip, Ira began another new project: his autobiography. Friends had wanted him to do this for a long time, but he was a modest man. When he finally decided to start writing, he wanted the book to be more about the gospel songs he sang, and their effect on people, than about his own life. He gave only the highlights of his life with Moody, giving few details about the many happenings while the two worked together. He concentrated on the gospel songs and their stories. But he did not include in the book many of the songs he himself had written.

A number of the songs had exciting stories related to them. Some had led a particular person to know the Lord. Others had a good anecdote about how they came to be written. Ira had told many of these "behind the scenes" stories when he was singing in the Moody and Sankey meetings. Now he was writing many of them down.

By the time the group arrived in France it was becoming obvious that war between the United States and Spain was getting closer. When the battleship *Maine*, while on a friendly visit, was sunk in the harbor of Havana, Cuba—then a Spanish colony—on February 15, 1898, 250 Americans were killed.

At home the people were angry about this "sneak attack," and calls for war increased. Ira was afraid that if war came, it might be hard to get home, since going by ship was the only way then to cross the Atlantic. He decided to take his family home before war could be declared.

The trip to the Holy Land was over. It had been a dream of Ira's for a long time, and he thought of it as "one of the most delightful experiences of my life."

Preparations for war were starting by the time Ira and his family got home. He visited an army camp in Tampa, Florida. Singing for a new generation of soldiers must have brought back memories of the months he had been in the army almost four decades earlier.

Although he was able to hold several meetings for the men, Ira was forced to turn down an invitation from Colonel Theodore Roosevelt, leader of the soon-to-be-famous Rough Riders. Ira had already scheduled another meeting.

The trip to the Holy Land had been just what Ira needed. Despite doing a lot of singing along the way, and working on his book, he had had a good rest. Seeing and walking in the places where Jesus had lived and taught had strengthened Ira's own faith and dedication. He was eager to get back to work with Moody.

As he waited in his Brooklyn home before meeting Moody, Ira heard that another evangelist, Gypsy Smith from England, would be holding services at a local church. Ira had heard of this man and his work for the Lord, and he called to ask if he could take the visitor for a drive the night before the first meeting.

As they rode along, Mr. Smith asked, "Do you

remember a time in 1874 when you and Mr. Moody came out to a gypsy camp in Epping Forest in England?"

"Yes. We went to see some of the men who had become Christians," Ira answered.

"And do you remember the little boy who climbed onto your carriage? You put your hand on his head and said, 'May God make you a preacher.'"

Ira may have forgotten the incident until then, but now he remembered.

"I am that little boy," Gypsy Smith said.

This incident was just another example of the results of Ira's life as a gospel singer, and it made him more eager than ever to meet with Moody and start working again.

When the two old friends met, they discussed the future. In the past, Ira's health had forced him to leave some of the Moody and Sankey campaigns early, or at least cut the number of times he sang solos. To keep gospel music in his meetings, Moody had had to make use of other singers as well.

In his own situation, Ira had begun to do more speaking along with his singing and had conducted some meetings on his own. Both men realized they did not have to work together all the time.

"If we go to different cities," one of them pointed out, "we can cover more ground and share the gospel with more people."

Because the two no longer held every meeting jointly, some people thought they had split up and were not friends any more. This was not true. They continued to hold some meetings together—and were always friends.

One of those meetings in which they combined their efforts was in Brooklyn, where Moody preached on "Mary and Martha." As it turned out, it was to be the last Moody and Sankey meeting. Of course, neither of them knew it then.

A few weeks later the two spent a Sunday afternoon together, with Ira walking Moody back to his hotel. Again, they did not realize it, but this would be their last "good-by" to each other. The years of working together to win people to Jesus were over.

Ira went on to a series of meetings in Canada. On his way home he stopped for a night in Rochester, New York, to hold a service. Ira called these services "Sacred Songs and Stories," telling many of the same stories that would later be in his autobiography.

In Rochester, Ira got a letter from Moody. It was written at Northfield on November 6, 1899, and was nine pages long! Moody talked about his work in Northfield and Chicago, starting the schools and Bible College. He asked Ira to meet him in New York City the next Wednesday at his hotel.

Immediately Ira sent a telegram, saying he would come on the night train and meet Moody in the morning. But when Ira got to the hotel, he learned that Moody had already left. The evangelist was headed for Kansas City for another round of meetings.

Although Ira knew his friend was not as strong

as he had once been, and that the doctors had told Moody he had to take things easier, he did not think of his long-time partner as being seriously ill. He expected to see him when the evangelist got back from Kansas City, and he went on with his own meetings.

Chapter

9

To England with "Sacred Songs and Stories"

IN KANSAS CITY, thousands of people again crowded the hall to hear Moody preach. But the evangelist knew he was weakening. He had never taken the English doctor's warning to cut back and take it easier and had kept working as hard as ever. For some time he had been having chest pains, but had not told anyone because he did not want to worry his family.

By the third day of the campaign, Moody knew he could not go on. The pain was severe, and his body was worn out. He wanted to go back to the Northfield home he loved.

Once the word of Moody's illness got out, the world held its breath. Would God spare this man who had brought so many to Christ? Or was his work on earth finished, and it was now time for his real homegoing?

Prayers were offered in many languages for Moody's healing. The best doctors were called in to try to save his life. For a time he seemed better, but it was not to be. On Friday, December 22, 1899, the world had its answer. Dwight L. Moody was dead. He had been able to talk to his family, and his last words to them were "God is calling me, and I must go."

A telegram was sent immediately to Ira, who quickly canceled the rest of his meetings. He hurried back to Northfield as quickly as possible, arriving the day before the funeral.

The final services for Moody were simple, as he had wished. They began with prayer in the parlor of his Northfield home about 10 in the morning of December 26, 1899.

After the service, the casket was put on a large, black-covered bier. It was carried by students from the Bible Institute in a procession to the Congregational Church. There the body lay in state and final services were held.

A sad Ira walked behind the students with other close friends and associates of Moody.

Moody was buried not far from his home on a knoll called Little Round Top—one of his favorite spots. He had led many meetings there during conferences at Northfield.

For Ira, Moody's death was a hard blow. It was like losing a brother. Even though his faith in God was as strong as ever, he knew he would miss this great man he had worked with—the man with whom he had shared so many good, as well as struggling, times. They had worked together for so many years, serving their Lord as an evangelistic team in countless meetings.

Ira had many fond memories of those days with Moody. Some were proof of his own singing ability and how much it had added to the services.

He remembered a night in Campbeltown, Scotland, when a drunken man lurched into the room and sat down. Moody was preaching, but the drunken man listened only a few minutes before he jumped up.

"Mr. Moody," he called out, "would you please stop for a bit? I want to hear Sankey sing 'The Ninety and Nine.'"

Ira had then sung the hymn that had become a favorite with people everywhere—and the drunken man went into the inquiry room to learn more about Christ and the free gift of salvation.

Another recollection that made Ira smile was from a time when he, along with another singer, and Moody were crossing the Connecticut River on a ferry. The ferry was moved ahead by the ferryman pulling forward on a wire stretched above the water. It was a slow trip, but took no fuel and was quiet.

Ira and the other man were singing various hymns, one after the other, while Moody helped the ferryman. After several songs Ira wondered why the ferry seemed to be moving even more slowly than usual. In fact, it seemed to move hardly at all.

He turned to see that Moody was pulling *back-*

ward on the wire as the ferryman pulled forward. It was the same as putting on the brakes! Moody had his own reasons for wanting the trip to last: he wanted to enjoy as much singing as possible, but he especially wanted the ferryman to hear them. The man was an old friend of Moody's but not a Christian.

To honor Moody and show his love and respect for him, Ira wrote a new hymn. This time he wrote both the words and the music, not just the music to accompany someone else's words, as he usually did. The hymn was "Out of the Shadows Into the Sunshine."

After the funeral in Northfield, Ira went back to his home in Brooklyn. He took part in several memorial services for his friend. The biggest one was at Carnegie Hall in New York City with 15,000 people coming. He sang the hymn he had written for Moody at this service.

Moody's death had a deep effect on Ira. His friend had been only a few years older than he was. If Moody was already dead, how many more years would he have to serve the Lord here?

Already many people, including newspaper writers, were saying that with Moody no longer alive, Ira's work was finished, too. But Ira was not willing to accept someone else's verdict on his life and work. If he was to stop singing and speaking, that order would have to come from God, not men!

During this period, Ira also took advantage of the time to record some of his songs. While Thomas Edison had invented the first phonograph some years before, it was not a practical machine for most uses until it was refined by others.

Now though, on wax cylinders it was possible to record songs and speech. Ira wanted people to be able to hear him sing whenever they wanted, and on cylinders his singing of the gospel would last for years.

He recorded several gospel hymns through Biglow & Main, where he was still president. Today very few of these recordings still exist, most being at the Moody Bible Institute in Chicago. The materials used then were not meant to stand up for a century of use, and the quality was low-grade compared to the CDs and tapes of today.

Among the hymns Ira recorded were "Beautiful City of God" and "Throw Out the Lifeline." If he ever made a recording of his most famous hymn, "The Ninety and Nine," it has been lost.

There were two other things Ira wanted to accomplish. "I want to finish my book. And I want to go back to England. It will prove to everyone that I am still working, and I can meet some of the old friends Mr. Moody and I made there before. It won't be a long trip, and it will be my last one there."

Ira planned to visit 30 cities, and his program would be called "Sacred Songs and Stories." He would sing a hymn and tell the story behind it, much as he was doing in his book. He would also get in a gospel message here and there in the program.

Ira and Fanny sailed for England in the fall of 1900. News of his coming had gone ahead and there were stacks of invitations for him to go to different places.

"It's not an evangelistic tour," Ira explained. "I just want to meet old friends."

Because this would be such a short trip, Ira could only visit the larger cities. A few days after the ship landed, he was in London. Here more than 20,000 people came out to hear him. Many said it was just like the old Moody and Sankey days.

When Ira stood up to speak, he could not do so for several minutes because of the applause. When he finally was able to talk to the crowd, it was an emotional time for him. He told the people that while he was glad to be there, he could not forget Moody who had been with him there before.

Ira went on to assure the crowd that he was the "original Sankey," and not his son, as some had reported. He then sat down at the organ and played and sang "When the Mists Have Rolled Away." After he finished, the hall was silent, and that was proof enough to Ira that his voice still had some of its old power and tone. He still had the ability to bring the words to life for the people listening. He also sang his theme song, "The Ninety and Nine." At the end of that special song many people in the audience were crying. It brought back memories to many of how it had influenced them or someone they knew to accept Christ's gift of salvation at a past Moody and Sankey meeting more than twenty-five years before.

Ira continued to travel around the British Isles. Everywhere he went his reception was the same as it had been in London. People crowded into the halls, and many had to be turned away.

"I'll sing to the others at an overflow meeting," he said. Despite knowing that this would put even more strain on his voice and his body, Ira could not bring himself to refuse to sing when people wanted to hear him.

He was in great demand and Ira was kindhearted. He could not turn down any request, and was soon doing much more than singing at his meetings. The people would not let him go, wanting to hear more, and wanting him to be with them. His strength began to weaken again.

"Cut your tour short," the doctors warned him. "Go back to America before your health breaks down completely."

Ira refused. "I'll sing to the end."

True to his word, Ira kept on with the tour until what the doctors had predicted came true. His health broke, and he had to return to the United States. He was now a frail, worn-out man, a semi-invalid in his Brooklyn home.

Chapter

10

Death and Beyond

THE WORLD welcomed the new century with bells and fireworks. People were trying to get used to saying and writing "1900" instead of "1800." And everyone knew that not one person celebrating would have much chance of seeing the year 2000.

Ira, although spending a lot more time resting, was still working hard on his book. He wanted it to be in perfect shape when it went to the printer. By 1901 it was nearly finished.

When the Sankeys decided to visit their friend Dr. John H. Kellogg at his Sanitarium in Battle Creek, Michigan, Ira decided to take the almost finished manuscript with him.

"It should be a quiet place to write," he told Fanny. "And I can finish it there."

The Sankeys were enjoying their visit when one night a piercing cry rang out: "Fire! Fire! Get out!"

The Sanitarium was in flames. It must have reminded Ira of the great Chicago fire and his experiences escaping it years before, when he had first started working with Moody.

Ira and Fanny raced outside, carrying nothing. All their belongings, including the one copy of his precious manuscript, were lost. The Sanitarium burned to the ground that night.

"It's over," Ira thought. He could not imagine trying to write the whole book over from the beginning!

"You have to do it," his friends told him. "You remember most of it, don't you?"

It took all Ira's will power and physical strength to make himself sit down at home and try to remember what he had said in the original manuscript. It helped that he had told these gospel stories many times in meetings before he sang the hymns. At last he did get the book rewritten and off to the publisher.

In 1901 Ira unknowingly sang in public for the last time. It was a special "Children's Sunday" at his church. The whole Sunday school decided to march to the home of one of the members to sing for him. Ira agreed to come along. There, the group sang hymns and Ira sang a solo, "Blest Be the Tie That Binds." Later, it somehow seemed appropriate that he had unconsciously ended his long public singing career with a song that stressed unity in Jesus. It was something he and Moody had always preached.

By the start of 1903, Ira had congestive glaucoma, an eye problem. It was painful and he knew it could lead to his becoming blind.

"There's pressure inside the eyeball, and it's destroying the optic nerve," his doctor told him. "But there is an operation that might help." Ira agreed to the surgery. The operation did ease his pain, but it did not stop the disease from getting worse and finally leaving him blind.

"It might not be permanent," his doctor said. "A complete rest might bring back some of your sight."

Ira and Fanny decided he should take his doctor's suggestion. They moved into the country and saw very few people. It was the complete rest Ira had been advised to have, but it did not help. He stayed blind. Eventually they moved back to Brooklyn.

At first Ira was discouraged because he could not see. He was depressed for a while, but he was basically a cheerful person, and after a few weeks that side of his personality came out again. He got back to playing the organ and determined to live the rest of his life the best he could.

Over the years Ira had made many friends around the world. One of the best was Fanny Crosby, the hymn writer. She had visited often at Northfield, taking part in some of the services there. At one time she had lived near the Sankeys in Brooklyn. While she no longer lived there, she came often to visit and pray with Ira.

While Fanny had worked with many composers for the thousands of hymns she had written over the years, Ira had put 237 of her poems to music.

Now that Ira was blind, the two had something

else in common. Fanny had been blind almost from birth, because the wrong prescription had been applied to her eyes when she was a small baby. She had known nothing but darkness all her life, yet her hymns were upbeat and optimistic, full of faith. She was the one person who could really understand and sympathize with Ira's pain and frustration at not being able to see any more.

Fanny may have reminded Ira of the time someone had tried to sympathize with her because she had never been able to see. Fanny had replied that she considered this a blessing. "Now the first face I will see is my Savior's."

We don't know what the two talked about during their hours together. It probably included remembering a lot of good times, like the summer of 1886 when Fanny was visiting. Ira had written a tune, but had no words to go with it.

"Why not write a poem for this tune?" he had asked Fanny.

At that moment Fanny did not think she could do it, but the next day, while the others were out for a drive, she wrote the words for "O Child of God."

The two friends may have laughed together about the time Fanny had gone to a Moody and Sankey meeting, apparently held in the late morning. There she heard the audience sing "O My Savior, Hide Me."

Fanny liked the song, and asked Ira, "Where did you get that piece?"

Ira, thinking she was joking, ignored her question. Before Fanny could ask him again, it was time to go to dinner, and they both forgot about the hymn. But Ira used it again in the afternoon services, and this time Fanny was determined to find out who had written the words that sounded so good to her.

"Mr. Sankey, you must tell me who wrote 'O My Savior, Hide Me.'"

Ira looked at her in surprise. "Don't you really remember who wrote it? You ought to; you're the guilty one!"

Other people also came to visit Ira in his home. Many had worked with him and Moody in some way in the revivals, either in Great Britain or America. Others were relatives like Essie McCurdy, Fanny's sister.

"Aunt Essie" came for long visits, the way people did in the days of slow and uncomfortable travel. She once stayed a year with her sister and Ira, handling a lot of Ira's massive correspondence and reading to him.

Not only individuals came to see Ira, but also groups. After a sunrise prayer service at a local church, about 1,000 people marched together to the Sankey home. The neighbors may have wondered what was going on as this crowd stood under Ira's window and sang some of his favorite songs for him.

Sometimes Ira would try to sing for a special guest, but he knew his voice was a mere shadow of what it had once been, and he did not sing often now.

However, not everyone who came to the Sankey house came as friends or to honor him. One night someone forced open a window at the back of the house while everyone was asleep. When the burglar, or burglars, got in, they stole about $1,000 worth of silverware and oil paintings. They cut the pictures from their frames to take with them.

As Ira's once big and robust body got weaker and thinner, his mind stayed as alert as ever. Now many visitors came to ask his opinion and to discuss religious matters.

One man, about to go back to England, asked, "Mr. Sankey, what would your message be to the English Christians? They remember you and love you."

"Tell them to stand fast by the old truths, cost them what it may, and contend earnestly for the faith once delivered to the saints," Ira told him. Then he added, "There will be no dark valley when Jesus comes, and we shall meet in the morning."

Another visitor who came during the last months of Ira's life reminisced with him about the times they had worked together. Then he asked, "Mr. Sankey, does the spirit of God and the power and truth of religion seem as clear and strong to you as when the tens of thousands were hanging on every word you said, and congratulating you on your popularity and success?"

Ira hesitated only a moment before saying, "It is more powerful. Then, there were so many distractions. God and I are together most of the time now."

A bright spot came for Ira in 1906 when his

rewritten autobiography and the story of the gospel hymns was finally published. It became a popular book, selling a lot of copies around the world and winning good comments from critics. Ira was pleased to be able to send autographed copies to some of his friends.

Ira knew, however, that his body was weaker, and he was extremely tired. He wanted to "go home" to Heaven where he would see Moody and the others he had worked with on earth.

On August 14, 1908, Ira died peacefully in his sleep. He had made all the arrangements for his funeral and had bought his cemetery lot. It was in a beautiful spot in Greenwood Cemetery, overlooking the ocean he had traveled on so often.

His gravestone mirrored his life's work with a bar of music on it, with "Good Night" and "God is Love" above and below it.

The funeral service was held in the Fayette Avenue Presbyterian Church near Ira's home in Brooklyn. He had joined this church because it was closer to his home, and easier for him to get to for Sunday morning services.

His funeral was one of the largest held in that church for years, but the service was simple and short, as he had requested. Ira was modest, even in death, wanting as little show as possible. A highlight came when Ira's cousin, an older man now, sang several of Ira's hymns, including "The Ninety and Nine."

Ira Sankey was a pioneer in gospel music, giving it that name. George C. Stebbins, another evangelistic singer of that day who had worked with Moody and Sankey, said: "He demonstrated in a most remarkable way . . . the power of the individual singing of the gospel, so that it has become a great ministry in evangelism."

Later gospel singers like Homer Rodeheaver, George Beverly Shea, and Gloria Gaither have all followed the path Ira broke for them.

"Second," Mr. Stebbins went on, "Sankey gave a distinctive name to evangelistic songs, which before had been called 'Sunday school songs.' 'Gospel hymns' was such an appropriate designation in the popular mind that the name has remained."

Memorial services for Ira Sankey were held around the world, as they had been for D.L. Moody. In England one minister compared the singer to Andrew, the disciple, ready to take second place to Simon Peter. He added, ". . . but doing it so beautifully that it stopped being second."

Billy Sunday, the evangelist then best known across America, led a service for Ira. Billy had sat and listened to Ira sing and now paid his respects not only to Ira but also to Fanny. He said, "No man has contributed to make the world better but that some woman has had a part in his accomplishments."

Fanny wanted something very special to keep Ira's memory alive, especially in New Castle. She decided on a "Memorial Window" for the First Methodist Church. The window would illustrate "The Ninety and Nine" in its various panels and circles. One of these would also show a man at an organ, while the large center area would have the Savior standing at the edge of a precipice and holding the lamb that had wandered. This window is still featured in the new church building built in the late 1990s.

The town of New Castle did not forget its favorite son, either, even after decades had gone by. In 1940, on the 100th anniversary of Ira's birth, the town and the Historical Society, with the help of Ira's few relatives still living, held a big celebration. They held another in 1990 on the 150th anniversary of his birth.

For the first of these celebrations, Moody's daughter-in-law asked a well-known radio singer of the day, Edward McHugh, to sing "The Ninety and Nine" over a national hookup. Mr. McHugh's voice was said to sound a lot like Ira's own, and through his singing the whole country was reminded of Ira's contribution to gospel music

Mrs. Moody also donated the Estey organ, and at this Centennial celebration a Sankey relative played the accompaniment for the singing of Ira's hymns.

Ira would have appreciated the Centennial celebration because it brought people from different churches together. Choirs from more than thirty churches took part. Moody and Sankey had always stressed that denominational differences were really slight. Knowing Christ as Savior was what counted. To them the "Church" was *all* Christians.

For this big meeting in 1940 special badges and

seats were reserved for the elderly and those who had known or heard Ira when he was alive.

In his remarks, the chief speaker, Dr. Will H. Houghton, the president of the Moody Bible Institute, summed up Ira's songs and music:

"His songs were personal, just as the Bible is personal."

Attention

Internet Users

Available on the internet is a four-page print-out, with pictures, A Brief History of Ira D. Sankey.

The web address is:
www.ilovehistory.com/irasankeyhistory.htm

Also available:

A cassette tape containing 16 Sankey songs performed by church choir singers at the 1990 Ira D. Sankey Sesquicentennial Celebration is available from the Lawrence County Historical Society, 408 N. Jefferson St., New Castle, PA 16101.

Price: $5.00 + $1.50 shipping

The Ninety and Nine

Elizabeth C. Clephane, 1830-1869

Melody by Ira D. Sankey, 1840-1908

The Ninety and Nine

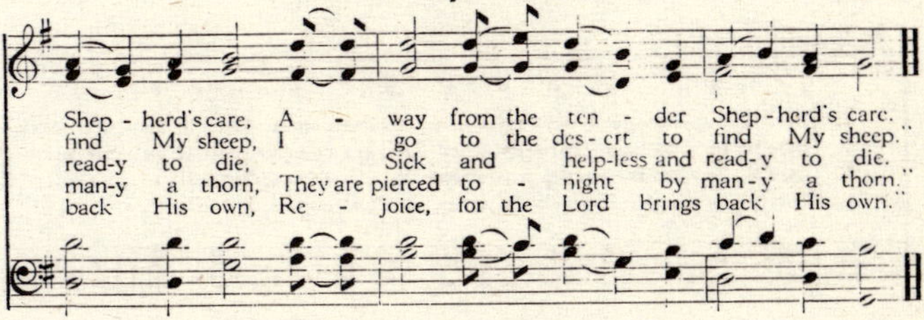

Hold the Fort

PHILIP P. BLISS, 1838-1876

PHILIP P. BLISS, 1838-1876

There'll Be No Dark Valley

WILLIAM O. CUSHING, 1823-1902

IRA D. SANKEY, 1840-1908

Acknowledgments

A hearty thank-you goes to many people for their help as I researched the life of Ira. D. Sankey, the first gospel singer.

The staffs of the Defiance College Library and the Defiance County Public Library, Defiance, Ohio—my hometown—helped locate books and articles dealing with the many campaigns of Dwight L. Moody and Mr. Sankey.

The First United Methodist Church of New Castle, Pennsylvania, allowed my husband and me to take photos of a portrait of Mr. Sankey and photocopied old photos to give me an idea of how some things would have looked to Mr. Sankey.

Walter Osborn, Reference Librarian at the Moody Bible Institute, took time from a busy schedule to answer many questions, both by mail and telephone, and to send photocopies of some material.

Beverly F. Zona, Executive Director of the Lawrence County (PA) Historical Society, helped me go through the Sankey Archives at its Museum in New Castle. The clippings, books, and pamphlets helped put many events into their proper time niche, while giving more details, along with a contemporary view of the singer.

This book was produced by the Christian Literature Crusade. We hope it has been helpful to you in living the Christian life. CLC is a literature mission with ministry in over 50 countries worldwide. If you would like to know more about us, or are interested in opportunities to serve with a faith mission, we invite you to write to:

Christian Literature Crusade
P.O. Box 1449
Fort Washington, PA 19034